KANSAS SPEEDWAY
5TH ANNIVERSARY
FIVE FOR THE FANS

F I V E   Y E A R   C O M M E M O R A T I V E

anthem
MOTORSPORTS

BOOK PRODUCTION

Publishing Firm:

Anthem Motorsports Inc.

Publisher:

Brian Weaver

Editor:

Katie Van Luchene

Corporate Creative Director:

Erin Benda

Art Director:

Todd Soligo

Contributing Writers:

Curt Cavin, Sammie Lukaskiewicz, Rick Peterson

KANSAS SPEEDWAY STAFF

Jeff Boerger - **President**

Kathy Borland - **Manager of Ticket Operations**

Latoria Chinn - **Guest Services Manager**

Darren Cook - **Director of Operations**

Randy Connor - **Public Relations Coordinator**

Joe Fowler - **Corporate Account Executive**

Kate Gregory - **Corporate Marketing Manager**

Jason Chaput - **Gate Operations Coordinator**

Lori Hampton - **Director of Accounting**

Ryan Hogue - **Manager of Group Sales**

Sammie Lukaskiewicz - **Public Relations Manager**

Tom Morelock - **Director of Ticket Operations**

Lisa Joyce - **Events and Hospitality Manager**

Greg Scott - **Facilities Superintendent**

Larry Shepek - **Security Manager**

Roy Skoglund - **Director of Marketing and Sales**

Stann Tate - **Director of Public Relations**

Published by Anthem Motorsports Inc., 7101 College Boulevard, Suite 1150, Overland Park, KS 66210. TEL: 913-894-6923, FAX: 913-894-6932, WWW.ANTHEMMOTORSPORTS.COM

CONTENTS

PREFACE

by Jeff Boerger
President, Kansas Speedway

When Kansas Speedway was completed in 2001, it became home to some of the fastest and fiercest competition in Kansas sports history.

Jeff Gordon, Dale Earnhardt Jr., Tony Stewart, Mark Martin, Bill Elliott – all of NASCAR's stars, then and now, competed at the track.

But getting the $250 million speedway built in just four short years also required speed. We achieved that speed from cooperation on the part of many people, companies and governmental entities.

The ingredients to Kansas Speedway's success included an owner with a clear vision, public officials with lofty-but-attainable goals, marketing partnerships with local, regional and international reach, and a design and construction team with the skills and determination to get the job done right and on time.

Lastly, it took race fans like you.

This book is a celebration of everyone involved – then and now – with Kansas Speedway, "The Track That Will Blow You Away!"

Kansas Speedway is owned by International Speedway Corporation of Daytona Beach, FL. ISC, best-known for its ownership of Daytona International Speedway (Florida), Talladega Superspeedway (Alabama) and Darlington Raceway (South Carolina), among others, had sought a state-of-the-art track for the Midwest for several years – and finally attained its goal in 1997.

Over the course of NASCAR's near-60 years, stock car racing has seen unprecedented growth. Sponsorships, superstar drivers, TV deals – America loves NASCAR, and more and more demand has been placed on new and improved venues.

New tracks were built across the country – especially out West – and new racing dates were added to the racing schedule.

With most of the speedways located in the Southeastern U.S. and some popping up in the West, ISC's vision was to bring big-time racing to the Midwest.

After an extensive search across the mid-United States, ISC finally chose Kansas City, KS. The decision was based mostly on its superior location at the junction of Interstate 70 and Interstate 435 in western Wyandotte County and the cooperation of state and local officials who had a vision, as well.

Former Kansas City, KS., Mayor and Chief Executive Officer of Wyandotte County's Unified Government Carol Marinovich and former Kansas Gov. Bill Graves worked tirelessly with ISC to build Kansas Speedway.

ISC hadn't built a racetrack from scratch since Talladega Superspeedway opened in 1969. ISC President Lesa France-Kennedy wanted to build a 75,000-seat motorsports palace so race fans could enjoy the best attributes of all the speedways. Some of

those attributes included superior sightlines, convenient ingress and egress and a streamlined flow from parking lots to the open and airy grandstand and its suites.

Public officials from the Unified Government of Wyandotte County and the state of Kansas have strived, along with ISC, from day one in 1997 to ensure the project's success.

The local officials and state leaders saw the speedway as a significant step toward bringing tourism and economic development to both the state and Wyandotte County.

As support for the facility and potential of what has now become the Village West area grew, the state, Unified Government and the Board of Public Utilities made significant improvements to the surrounding roadways and infrastructure of the area. Interstate 70, State Avenue, 110th Street and New Jersey Street were all reconstructed to accommodate the increased traffic.

HNTB Corporation, the DLR Group and Turner Construction Company worked closely with ISC and public officials during design and construction of the facility. HNTB took the lead in the planning and design, along with the DLR Group and nearly 45 other consultants, doing anything and everything from soils investigations to audiovisual work.

Turner Construction took the lead in construction with more than 150 contractors working to complete the project by the target date – spring of 2001.

In all, the project created more than 2,000 construction jobs with a combined payroll of more than $50 million.

And that was during construction phase alone.

FOUR SEASONS OF DRAMA

BY RICK PETERSON

IF YOU KNOW AUTO RACING, YOU KNOW KANSAS SPEEDWAY. AND ALTHOUGH THE SPEEDWAY IS BEST KNOWN AS A 1.5-MILE TRI-OVAL, THERE ARE MANY OTHER COMPONENTS THAT HAVE HELPED ESTABLISH THE KANSAS CITY, KANSAS FACILITY AS ONE OF RACING'S MAJOR VENUES IN JUST FOUR SHORT SEASONS.

Kansas Speedway is about the fans, who lined up for tickets before the facility was even built and who have turned out in sellout numbers since the track opened in the spring of 2001.

That fan support justified expansion from 75,000 seats in 2001 to a capacity of approximately 82,000 for 2005, with more expansion planned the future.

The speedway is about the drivers, with scores of the world's best converging in Kansas City in the track's first four seasons, including nine NASCAR Winston and NEXTEL Cup champions and seven Indianapolis 500 winners. The list includes 2004 NEXTEL Cup champion Kurt Busch and 2004 Indy 500 champ Buddy Rice.

In its first four seasons, the speedway has already had its share of dramatic finishes, including Rice's victory over teammate Vitor Meira in the 2004 IRL event, a finish that ranked as the second-closest in IRL history. Four-time NASCAR champ Jeff Gordon, a two-time winner in Kansas, also has a nail-biting speedway victory to his credit, winning the first Cup event in 2001 by less than a half-second over Ryan Newman, who tasted victory at the speedway himself in 2003.

Kansas Speedway is about the economic boost it's provided for Kansas City and Wyandotte County, with the speedway generating about $150 million in tourism in its inaugural season alone.

The Village West development, 400 acres adjacent to the track, includes a minor league baseball team as well numerous other lodging, dining and retail establishments.

And as successful as Kansas Speedway has been, there seems to be little doubt that even more prosperous times are still ahead.

Kansas Speedway is not yet close to its maximum seating capacity, and it's not out of the question for the track to eventually reach 150,000 seats.

There is also the possibility that the track might someday add lights, which would afford fans the opportunity to watch night-time racing, particularly during Kansas's sweltering summer heat.

"As great of facility as it is, because of its success it will breed further success," said former Kansas governor Bill Graves.

THE BEGINNING

When International Speedway Corporation began scouting for Midwest locations, it seemed to find an ideal match in Kansas City, KS.

"I've now had some opportunities (on the ISC board) to observe how this process works, and quite clearly there are some locations that you might say open their arms and roll out the red carpet a little more enthusiastically than others," said former Kansas governor Bill Graves. "Kansas City, Kansas clearly made a very strong impression on ISC as a community that wanted to have a speedway. That goes a long, long, long way in ultimately getting a project like that done."

Graves signed a bill into law in February of 1998 that paved the way for the speedway and construction began on the 1,300-acre site later that year.

The three-year construction project reached its zenith with the track's opening in the spring of 2001, but expansion projects have been ongoing, with the track's seating capacity increasing from 75,000 in 2001 to 82,000 for 2005.

"It was very easy to understand how this was going to be a win, win, win, win situation," Graves said. "It was going to be good for Kansas City, Kansas. It was going to be good for the state of Kansas. It was going to be good for International Speedway Corporation and it was going to be good for the legions of motorsport racing fans who lived in the Midwest."

THE FANS

When it became evident in the late 1990s that Kansas Speedway would become a reality, Midwest fans started lining up for tickets. They haven't stopped since, packing the speedway for the first four Indy Racing League and NASCAR Cup events and also piling up big attendance figures for NASCAR Craftsman Truck Series and ARCA RE/MAX events.

"We put our money down (for tickets) when it was still dirt," said Belton, MO fan Linda Schoor. "What I remember is the first year when you were actually seeing a Cup race in person for the first time and to watch 43 drivers come around and just watch that green flag fly, and the race is on and you're actually watching it. That's probably the most exciting thing and the one that sticks out clearest of any of the races."

"It was wonderful to get something that close – too close to where you just can't not go," said Lynda Bell of Kansas City, MO.

Drivers fell in love with Kansas Speedway almost as quickly as the fans, particularly drivers from the Midwest.

"At that time [of her first Speedway appearance], this is what I said I felt like: It's like being the little local band that plays in the local bar and then all of a sudden gets to go play like at Sandstone [now the Verizon Amphitheater]," said Busch Series driver Jennifer Cobb of Kansas City, KS. "It was just all of a sudden from the little tracks to a national audience."

Emporia, KS native Clint Bowyer agreed.

"I think Kansas Speedway – with the ARCA race and even the Busch race and the truck race – gives people a goal, and they can run those races. It gives these local racers at least a taste of the bigtime and, if nothing else, just being able to say that they did it. I think it's just a big inspiration to all of us, just having it there."

THE DRIVERS

Racing's biggest names have already made Kansas Speedway a regular stopping point, with the roll call including former Winston Cup champions Terry Labonte, Bill Elliott, Rusty Wallace, Jeff Gordon, Dale Jarrett, Bobby Labonte, Tony Stewart and Matt Kenseth, as well as last year's inaugural NEXTEL Cup champ, Kurt Busch.

All nine Indy Racing League champions have raced in Kansas, including Indianapolis 500 champions Al Unser Jr., Buddy Lazier, Eddie Cheever Jr., Kenny Brack, Helio Castroneves, Gil de Ferran and Buddy Rice.

Eleven NASCAR Busch Series champs have raced in Kansas, including 2004 champ Martin Truex Jr., as well as all seven champions in the NASCAR Craftsman Truck Series and most of the premier names in the ARCA RE/MAX Series, including the series' winningest driver, Frank Kimmel.

Columbia, MO's Carl Edwards was the first area driver to taste victory at Kansas Speedway, winning the 2004 NASCAR Craftsman Truck Series event.

"The neatest thing that I think has ever happened to me in my career, as far as a feeling from fans and feeling a crowd's energy, was when we won that truck race there," Edwards said. "I remember the last caution period after we had just passed for the lead if, I remember correctly, and we rolled around under caution.

"I looked over and it seemed like everybody was standing on their feet screaming and yelling. That was pretty motivating. At that point I felt like I had 75,000 friends there, and that was a pretty cool feeling."

"**What I remember** is the first year when you were
actually seeing a Cup race in person for the first time
and to watch 43 drivers come around and just watch that green flag fly,
and the race is on and you're actually watching it."

THE RACES

Jeff Gordon's victory by 0.413 of a second over Ryan Newman in the inaugural NASCAR Cup event set the tone for dramatic Kansas Speedway finishes.

And Gordon's 2001 victory would seem almost like a runaway compared to Buddy Rice's win over teammate Vitor Meira in the 2004 July 4th Indy Racing League event.

After a 10-lap, side-by-side battle at the end of the race, Rice won by 0.0051 of a second over Meira in a finish that left most people in the grandstands and pits, including Rahal Letterman Racing owner Bobby Rahal, unsure of who had won the race.

"From where I stood, I thought Vitor had won it, but I was happy either way," Rahal said. "I didn't care. All I knew was we were one-two."

The finish was the second-closest in Indy Racing League history.

There have also been other dramatic racing moments at the speedway, including a 2002 turn-two crash that took Sterling Marlin out of the NASCAR championship chase and a 2004 late-race Busch Series tangle between Tony Stewart and Joe Nemechek, which took race leader Stewart out of the race and catapulted Nemechek into victory lane. Nemechek would make the same trip the following day, doubling up in the NASCAR NEXTEL Cup race.

THE GROWTH

The 400-acre Village West area outside Kansas Speedway has rivaled the success of the track, spearheading economic development in Kansas City, KS and Wyandotte County.

"When we went for the speedway, we weren't simply going for the speedway, which we knew would be a very positive addition to our community and something that we would be very, very proud of," said Carol Marinovich, mayor and chief executive officer of the Unified Government of Wyandotte County and Kansas City, KS. "We knew the speedway would be the spark to ignite and generate development next to it."

The result has been the arrival of the minor league baseball team Kansas City T-Bones as well as Cabela's, Nebraska Furniture Mart, Applebee's Neighborhood Grill and Bar, Great Wolf Lodge, Chateau Avalon, Hampton Inn and numerous other successful businesses.

Expected to open in the fall of 2005 is The Legends at Village West, a 750,000-square-foot shopping and entertainment destination.

"We were hoping for this kind of growth around us, but had no idea it would come so quickly," said Kansas Speedway President Jeff Boerger. "Development of this kind usually takes years. With this project, it was amazing how quickly businesses signed on."

THE FUTURE

Will Kansas Speedway top the 100,000 mark in seating capacity? Will there eventually be night racing?

It's impossible to say, but it would also be foolish to rule out such possibilities.

After all, most fans never thought they'd see a major track in their home area in their lifetime, let alone the overwhelming success that Kansas Speedway has become.

"I never thought it would come to fruition," said Keith Hughes of Olathe, KS. "When I first heard that it might happen I went 'yeah, right.' "

Larry Larson of Wichita, KS had similar thoughts.

"I always figured that Kansas would never get one, but we finally did and that's quite a thrill," Larson said.

Even some of auto racing's biggest names were surprised and happy to see the Midwest become a major player in the sport.

"We were never close to the Midwest," NASCAR legend Richard Petty said in 2001. "People would say 'you don't have a race within 650 miles of me.'

"Now we have a chance to say thanks to all our old friends and make some new ones, and that's not bad."

KANSAS SPEEDWAY
FUELING TOURISM,
VILLAGE WEST
BY SAMMIE LUKASKIEWICZ

STATE AND LOCAL OFFICIALS ARE FINDING **KANSAS SPEEDWAY IS THE ECONOMIC ENGINE DRIVING DEVELOPMENT IN THE REGION.**

According to an economic impact survey commissioned by the track in 2001, Kansas Speedway alone generated about $150 million in tourism in its inaugural season.

But state and local officials are hoping for – and continue to see – much more. Yes, the speedway attracts race fans from all across the country twice a year. But it's what the speedway has done outside the racing world that is making people take notice.

When the speedway was built, state, city and county officials believed it would act as a catalyst to jump-start development and growth in the region.

And that it did.

Adjacent to Kansas Speedway, just across State Avenue and France Family Drive, sits a 400-acre development parcel owned by the Unified Government, the governing partnership between Kansas City, KS, and its county, Wyandotte County.

When International Speedway Corporation approached the Unified Government to build Kansas Speedway, Marinovich had the vision to turn 400 acres across from the speedway into a tourism district.

Village West was born.

Comprising Village West are national companies the likes of which Wyandotte County, the Kansas City metro area and the state have never seen.

Phase One of the Tourism District included Cabela's, Nebraska Furniture Mart, Applebee's Neighborhood Grill and Bar, Great Wolf Lodge, Chateau Avalon and Hampton Inn.

A minor-league baseball team also relocated to Village West to a brand new, state-of-the-art stadium across the street from Kansas Speedway. Wyandotte County has been the home of the Kansas City T-Bones ever since.

Ted's Montana Grill, W.J. McBride's, Sheridan's Frozen Yogurt and Jimmy Buffett's Cheeseburger in Paradise soon opened, and a thriving tourism industry in Wyandotte County was born.

"We were hoping for this kind of growth around us, but had no idea it would come so quickly," speedway President Jeff Boerger said. "Development of this kind usually takes years. With this project, it was amazing how quickly businesses signed on."

Before development began, the 400 acres known as Village West used to generate only $15,000 a year in property taxes.

Today, an estimated 4,000 jobs will be created upon eventual completion of Village West, and more than $10 million in property taxes and $26 million in sales tax revenues will be infused into the local economy.

The respected Kansas City business publication, *Ingram's*, recently reviewed the "Thirty Biggest Deals of the Past 30 Years in the Kansas City Metro" and included Kansas Speedway and Village West development. *Ingram's* reported:

"The impact was both immediate and electric. The $200 million in construction along the I-435 corridor generates more than $300 million annually. Shrewd planning by the Unified Government also set the stage for retail and other development nearly equal to the speedway itself. Overnight, KCK and western Wyandotte County became one of the hottest growth areas of the region. The timing was dramatic. KCK and Wyandotte County had been losing residents because of the lack of retail services and other amenities. That same lack of business hampered government services by lowering sales tax revenues and forcing up tax rates. The result was the kind of downward cycle that is hard to reverse."

In 2004, Village West generated $5.5 million in property taxes – property taxes which are helping pay for schools, state programs and other government services.

Village West's development company, RED Development, has also broken ground on The Legends, an outdoor shopping and entertainment district inside the tourism district. The total investment on The Legends is $246 million – $132 million in private investment dollars and $114 million in public investment through an innovative economic development tool known as STAR Bonds.

STAR Bonds, which helped build Kansas Speedway, use newly generated sales tax dollars produced by the development to help pay for the development.

The state passed STAR Bond legislation, an innovative development measure, in the late 1990s to attract new growth for the state.

The Legends portion of Village West is estimated to generate $4.2 million a year in new property taxes, with an estimated $1.5 million of that new money going to public schools.

By the time the development is completed, Village West will be generating about $7 million in property taxes annually and attracting more than 10 million visitors annually. Most of the tourists will come from more than 200 miles away.

"The speedway has done everything that we envisioned it would do to the tourism district – an unwavering vision of what could, should and would happen next to the speedway," Marinovich said.

When all phases of Village West are complete, the development will amount to more than $400 million, with projected annual sales of more than $440 million.

This is an economic engine that will bring year-round economic activity to a county that didn't even have a movie theater.

"What we're doing here is not just creating opportunities for folks to come and leave their money – which is one of the things we do like – and then they go away and then they come back. But we are also creating opportunities for Kansas to have good, decent, quality jobs," said former Kansas Lt. Gov. Gary Sherrer, integral to the process of bringing Kansas Speedway to Kansas City, KS.

"When all of this comes together, the synergy of this area, the track, indeed, the wonderful track. Nothing or no one could deliver more on its promise than this track has – this wonderful track."

The Village West development has also sparked a major building boom in Wyandotte County. Single family housing permits hit a 40-year high in 2003, with 433 new home permits issued. The total value of new construction permits in 2003 was $114 million.

Today, Kansas Speedway seats about 82,000 and plans are to eventually expand – just like the growth and tourism of Wyandotte County.

SOARING TROPHY
A WORK OF ART

BY SAMMIE LUKASKIEWICZ

A TROPHY IS THE NORM AT SOME TRACKS.
AT KANSAS SPEEDWAY, THE WINNER RECEIVES A WORK OF ART.

Kansas Speedway's winner's trophy is aptly called "Soaring." The piece was designed by renowned Canadian sculptor May Marx.

Each sculpture is cast in solid bronze, polished to perfection and individually signed. Only race winners at Kansas Speedway receive the trophy. The speedway displays a larger version of the trophy with each of the past race winners' names inscribed on the base in the administrative offices.

"I wanted the trophy to evoke conversation. That's probably one of the biggest reasons why Soaring was chosen," said Stann Tate, director of public relations for the race track.

Another reason: Tate wanted the piece to be synonymous with a win at Kansas Speedway.

"It's kind of like the Oscar or the Stanley Cup," he said. "Both are recognizable to everyone, and that's how I want people to associate our track trophy."

"... THROUGH THE ABSTRACT FORMS OF MY SCULPTURES I CAN EXPRESS IDEAS, EXPERIENCES AND EMOTIONS IN A WAY THAT TRANSCENDS THE LIMITATIONS OF WORDS."
– MAY MARX,
SCULPTOR OF KANSAS SPEEDWAY'S WINNER'S TROPHY

Only two other institutions – one in upstate New York and one in Europe – have Soaring. But Kansas Speedway now owns exclusive rights to the piece, and copies will only be given to race winners.

Most teams purchase replica copies of the trophy following a win at the track. They're proudly displayed in their race shops or at their homes.

Joe Nemechek, after winning Kansas Speedway's NASCAR NEXTEL Cup Series and NASCAR Busch Series events in October 2004, quickly purchased copies of the trophy to display in his team's MB2 NASCAR Busch Series race shop in North Carolina.

Another trophy is proudly displayed on his fireplace mantle at home.

"It's such a unique piece of artwork – not like any other trophy on the circuit."

Four-time NASCAR champion Jeff Gordon has hundreds of trophies in his collection – each one of them special.

But Kansas Speedway's is distinctive, he said.

"Kansas Speedway's trophy is a real work of art and reflects the progress that tracks and this sport have made over the past 40 or 50 years. I applaud

them for using something extraordinary to reward a win. And every time I look at the trophy, I'm reminded of being the inaugural winner at the track – and that's always a special feeling. Having two of the trophies makes it that much better."

Marx came up with Soaring after watching a television program about hanggliding.

"I came to work the next day and thought how wonderful it must be to fly through the air like that," she said. "The forms just seem to flow and soar."

Marx is a leading contemporary artist whose innovative works have been acclaimed worldide. Working solely in bronze, her expressive limited edition and commissioned sculptures are in galleries throughout North America and Europe.

Some 35 years ago, Marx chanced upon a clay modeling demonstration, and it changed her life forever. What was initially a fascination has translated into a passionate involvement. She has spent her life creating exceptional sculptures and furthering the art community through her teaching, her

writing and her contributions to the Board of Visual Arts and The Sculptors' Society of Canada. Her talent has earned her many awards along with an international reputation as an artist of innovative works.

Born in Toronto, Marx studied art at the Ontario College of Art and Central Technical School. Initially dividing her time between teaching and practicing art, she left teaching to commit full time to her own work, sculpture, printmaking and painting.

She creates sculptures that capture the essence of human relationships in abstract forms. In addition to developing new sculptures for private and corporate art collections, Marx continues to explore fresh directions in her work and has designed original pieces for Ford, AT&T and Chrysler.

But it is of Kansas Speedway's trophy that she is most proud.

"I've seen the kind of trophies that are used, and I really have always had the thought that when people win something, it should be something really beautiful and make people feel an emotion," she said. "That's why I'm extremely proud Kansas Speedway has the courage to step forward and use the piece."

Marx designed the sculpture so it would be touchable, she said. It has been treated with a special lacquer to keep it from tarnishing when touched.

KANSAS SPEEDWAY SPEEDWAY WINNERS

NASCAR NEXTEL CUP SERIES

2001 - JEFF GORDON
2002 - JEFF GORDON
2003 - RYAN NEWMAN
2004 - JOE NEMECHEK

NASCAR BUSCH SERIES

2001 - JEFF GREEN
2002 - JEFF BURTON
2003 - DAVID GREEN
2004 - JOE NEMECHEK

ARCA RE/MAX SERIES

2001 - JASON JARRETT
2002 - FRANK KIMMEL
2003 - SHELBY HOWARD
2004 - RYAN HEMPHILL

NASCAR CRAFTSMAN TRUCK SERIES

2001 - RICKY HENDRICK
2002 - MIKE BLISS
2003 - JON WOOD
2004 - CARL EDWARDS

IRL INDYCAR SERIES

2001 - EDDIE CHEEVER
2002 - AIRTON DARE
2003 - BRYAN HERTA
2004 - BUDDY RICE

IRL INFINITI PRO SERIES

2002 - A.J. FOYT IV
2003 - MARK TAYLOR
2004 - THIAGO MEDEIROS

CART DAYTON INDY LIGHTS CHAMPIONSHIP

2001 - KRISTIAN KOLBY

NASCAR WINSTON WEST SERIES

2001 - FRANK KIMMEL

2001

Banquet 400

Mr. Goodcents 300

KANSAS INDY 300

Aventis RACING FOR KIDS 100 At Kansas Speedway

O'Reilly AUTO PARTS 250

BPU 200 Kansas City, Kansas

57

CATCHING THE DREAM

BY RICK PETERSON

FOR CARL EDWARDS THE FEELING WAS LIKE HE HAD JUST MADE SOME NEW FRIENDS — THOUSANDS AND THOUSANDS OF THEM. JENNIFER JO COBB FELT A LITTLE LIKE A ROCK STAR AFTER MAKING IT TO RACING'S BIG STAGE. AND, AFTER YEARS OF DRIVING PAST KANSAS SPEEDWAY TO RACE AT OTHER TRACKS, CLINT BOWYER REALIZED THAT DREAMS DO COME TRUE. ALL THREE MIDWEST DRIVERS HAVE FORMED THEIR OWN DISTINCT MEMORIES OF THE 1.5-MILE KANSAS CITY, KANSAS FACILITY AND READILY AGREE THAT KANSAS SPEEDWAY HAS BEEN A SPECIAL PLACE IN THEIR LIVES AND THEIR CAREERS SINCE IT OPENED IN 2001.

"It's pretty amazing," said Edwards, who competes in NASCAR's premier series, the NEXTEL Cup Series, for Roush Racing. "I tell people I remember when they first started the project and first broke ground and it was a huge story, even in Columbia, MO, where I'm from. At that point I was racing at the local race tracks and you're dreaming about getting to race at a track like that.

"To me it was something that was really neat. It brought big-time racing so close to home that it really just made that dream something tangible, to be able to drive by that track and see it right there. It was the first major race track I had ever seen, so that was pretty cool."

Bowyer, an Emporia, KS native who races in the NASCAR Busch Series for Richard Childress Racing, echoed Edwards' sentiments.

"Driving by it while it was being built, going to a dirt track five miles up the road (Lakeside Speedway), you stopped and it gave you something to dream about," Bowyer said. "It gave you a goal and for sure something to dream about.

"I think it's just been a big inspiration to all of us, just having it there."

Cobb grew up a stone's throw from the ground where Kansas Speedway now stands. And although she knew in her heart that she would make it to racing's bigtime some day, she gives her home track credit for providing an impetus for her climb from local racer to driving instructor for the Richard Petty Driving Experience to the ARCA RE/MAX Series and now to Busch.

"I wouldn't say that this wouldn't have happened without the track, but I would say that the race track has been a very, very important part in the development of my career and the speed of it," Cobb said. "It would have taken me years probably to work up to the ARCA Series.

"It definitely fast-forwarded it and helped it. This has been my dream since I was eight years old – it was going to happen – but it for sure would not have happened this efficiently and quickly as it has happened."

All three drivers have their personal highlights that the speedway has provided in its short four-season history, including Edwards's win in the NASCAR Craftsman Truck Series O'Reilly Auto Parts 250 on July 3, 2004. That win made him the first area driver to visit Kansas Speedway's victory lane.

In that race, Edwards crashed in turn two on the very first lap of the race and battled his way back through the field to take the lead.

"The neatest thing that I think has ever happened to me in my career, as far as a feeling from fans and feeling a crowd's energy, was when we won that truck race there," Edwards said. "I remember the last caution period, after we had just passed for the lead, and we rolled around under caution.

KANSAS SPEEDWAY

"I looked over and it seemed like all over the grandstands everybody was standing on their feet screaming and yelling. That was pretty motivating."

– Carl Edwards

"I looked over and it seemed like all over the grandstands everybody was standing on their feet screaming and yelling. That was pretty motivating. At that point, I felt like I had 75,000 friends there, and that was a pretty cool feeling."

Although a lot of time has passed since that victory, neither Edwards or his fans have forgotten the moment.

"When I come back home, I see so many familiar faces and I get to talk to so many people that I've known for so long. And the neatest part about that win is that now I run into people all the time and I've had hundreds of people tell me, 'Man, I was at that race that you won in Kansas,' " Edwards said. "To talk to people who were there and to see their photographs from the grandstands, it almost seems surreal."

Cobb's biggest speedway memory to date is the day she lined up for her first career ARCA start.

She said she felt a lot of emotions that day – nervousness, anticipation, excitement and a tremendous amount of pride.

"It was just all of a sudden from the little tracks to a national audience."

Now Cobb will be performing on a regular basis on that national level, but she said she'll never forget that day that helped launch it all.

"It was way more overwhelming than my first Busch race. Way more so," Cobb said. "To date, that's the biggest. That first year it was such a big deal. The attendance was great and they put us all in a truck and had us ride around the track and wave to the crowd. That was all happening for the first time for me, all the pre-race festivities.

"And then when I started that race, it was the first time that I'd had that much horsepower under me. It was absolutely a very exciting and overwhelming day. And to finish it inside the top 20 – most people didn't think I'd even finish it – it was just really a great day, a great starting point for the rest of my career."

Bowyer, who shared a Busch ride with Kevin Harvick in 2004, made his Kansas Speedway debut in the October 9, 2004 Busch race, but it was something that happened a day earlier on the speedway's Fan Walk Stage that made that weekend unforgettable.

On that day, with a throng of Bowyer's family, friends and fans looking on, Childress announced that Bowyer would drive the No. 2 ACDelco car on a full-time basis in 2005.

"To be able to announce that at my home track, which is special to me to begin with, was probably the coolest thing that's happened to me," Bowyer said.

That day proved to Bowyer that all his years of hard work had finally started to pay off.

"For Richard to give me even a chance and an opportunity at what he did was a longshot. And I'm glad it worked out, but I think it shows to racers out there that it can happen. It gives them some sort of aspiration to work at it and keep working and not just stick around that local level, but try to get in a touring series and work their way up," Bowyer said.

"What I think my thing shows is that you can do it the hard way. If you don't have the money to back you up, there's still racers out there that do it the hard way."

Edwards, Bowyer and Cobb have now all graduated to racing's fast lane and all three agree that Kansas Speedway and other tracks in the Midwest will provide opportunities for a host of other area racers to follow in their footsteps.

Eudora's Chase Austin is well on his way to that point, after the 15-year-old signed a contract in late 2004 to join Hendrick Motorsports' driver developmental program for 2005.

"I think Kansas Speedway — with the ARCA race and even the Busch race and the truck race — gives people a goal, and they can run those races,"

- Clint Bowyer

"I thought it would take a lot longer, it would take more years and stuff like that, me driving more and getting more recognition," Austin said during a Kansas Speedway visit in October 2004. "When I was young it wasn't even on my mind.

"I saw NASCAR on TV, and I didn't know if it was something put up like professional wrestling and stuff like that that's fake. I didn't imagine it would be anything like this."

Cobb said that the success of Midwest drivers just proves that the area is now a major player in the auto racing industry.

"If you look five, 10 years ago at the bulk of the races, it was definitely in the Southeast," Cobb said. "Now if you look at maybe a central point and went six to eight hours around wherever the bulk of the races are, that is much closer to Kansas City.

"I think all of those tracks that opened up – Kansas and Chicagoland and even Texas and there's some Busch races in St. Louis – the racing geography is definitely migrating closer to us."

That, according to Edwards, can only be a good thing.

"As the sport becomes more mainstream, more folks are excited about going racing, and that makes for more car owners and more teams at all different levels. I think that's part of the reason why you're seeing guys like Clint Bowyer and Jamie McMurray (Joplin, MO) and myself getting these opportunities; guys that are from our area.

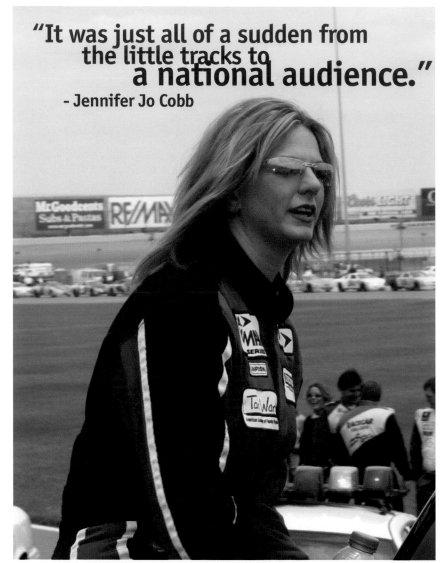

"It was just all of a sudden from the little tracks to a national audience."
- Jennifer Jo Cobb

"For a long time, after Kenny Schrader and Rusty Wallace and those guys, there weren't many drivers to come out of this area. For me, personally, the St. Louis and Kansas speedways helped a lot because those were tracks that Mike Mittler, the guy I was driving the truck for, could afford to go to and find sponsorship for."

Although not every area driver who gets a chance to drive at Kansas Speedway will end up as a regular in Busch or NEXTEL Cup, Bowyer said that it gives them that chance.

"I think Kansas Speedway – with the ARCA race and even the Busch race and the truck race – gives people a goal, and they can run those races," Bowyer said. "It gives these local racers at least a taste of the bigtime and, if nothing else, just being able to say that they did it."

And Bowyer, Cobb, Edwards and McMurray are ample evidence that you might just catch lightning in a bottle.

"If they happen to run good with little backing or money behind them, of course that looks good and catches the eye of a race car owner," Bowyer said.

"I went down to an ARCA race in Nashville with next to nothing and got a dream come true out of it."

And although Edwards beat him to the punch when he became the first area winner at Kansas Speedway, Bowyer still has hopes of adding another speedway highlight if he could become the first native Kansan to post a victory.

"I plan on it," Bowyer said.

CHANGING FACE
OF MOTORSPORTS STARTED IN KANSAS

BY SAMMIE LUKASKIEWICZ

IN A SPORT FUELED MOSTLY BY FAST CARS, IT'S THE DRIVERS, SPONSORS, NEW TRACKS AND EVEN NEWER FANS THAT ARE CHANGING THE FACE OF MOTORSPORTS THESE DAYS.

Young drivers, savvy sponsors and state-of-the-art facilities are helping drive the growth of NASCAR and the IRL.

Is there a changing face in motorsports today?

"There's a lot of change going on," said NASCAR NEXTEL Cup Series driver Kevin Harvick. "Not only is there change among the ages of the drivers, there's a change among the age of the crew chiefs, there's a change among the way the teams work. There's a lot of change, especially in NASCAR."

The younger and more diverse fan base that NASCAR and the Indy Racing League are generating and constantly striving to increase can be directly related to the younger, hipper drivers today and their demographic-conscious sponsors, according to Jim Hunter, NASCAR's vice president of corporate communications.

As a result, new tracks and new sponsors have been key to the growth.

Cell phones. New sponsors. Exciting TV packages. Everything about motorsports screams younger generation.

And the drivers themselves seem to be billboards for a new youth movement that is sweeping motorsports today. Just looking at 2004's major series champions says it all: NASCAR NEXTEL Cup Series champion Kurt Busch was only 26 when he was crowned. His IRL counterpart Tony Kanaan was 29.

"You have these great younger drivers like Dale Earnhardt Jr., Ryan Newman, Jimmie Johnson and Kurt Busch and they automatically bring a whole new fan base to NASCAR," Hunter said. "They're young, they've been on the covers of magazines that the young people read that are not usually associated with racing. They're the faces that young men and young women can identify with."

Earnhardt Jr. has been featured in People and Playboy magazines – two publications with readers at each end of the demographic spectrum. And other drivers such as the IRL's Dario Franchitti, Dan Wheldon and Helio Castroneves look more like GQ cover models than their former racing counterparts.

NASCAR's four-time champions Jeff Gordon hosted "Saturday Night Live" in 2003.

This diversity bodes well for NASCAR and IRL, who are constantly striving to attract that elusive demographic of men ages 18-35 and women.

While veteran brand sponsors such as R.J. Reynolds and Unocal are slowly leaving the sport, they're quickly being replaced by hip names such as NEXTEL, America Online, Red Bull and Drakkar Noir to target that demographic.

"A driver like Dale Earnhardt Jr. or Ryan Newman or Jimmie Johnson will

automatically attract that young demographic that companies are looking for," Hunter said. "They are these great drivers that aren't afraid to pass, or to take a risk that their fathers or other drivers before them may not have made.

"So more than keeping old fans, these drivers seem to be making new fans."

That fan base, through sponsorships, also bodes well for race tracks. Kansas Speedway opened in 2001 to sold-out crowds.

Each year since, the track announced it was sold out quicker than previous years.

WELCOME RACE FANS!

NASCAR has never seen a reception during an inaugural weekend as it saw in Kansas City, KS, in 2001.

That excitement carried over to 2002 … and then again in 2003 and 2004.

"Believe it or not, there are some places that don't like NASCAR in their communities. But not Kansas City. Never, ever has NASCAR been welcomed like we were in Kansas," Hunter said.

In a letter to Kansas Speedway and local and state leaders in 2001, NASCAR President Mike Helton wrote: "We look forward to returning to Kansas Speedway, the city of Kansas City, Kansas, and the great state of Kansas. The race track, the city and region are first-rate additions to our schedules. Just as we were welcomed, we at NASCAR want to reciprocate and welcome Kansas Speedway, knowing it will be an integral part of the future growth of NASCAR auto racing."

The letter marked the first time NASCAR has congratulated a community and a race track on a successful event, Hunter said.

"The track, the fans, the community. Everything made it a great weekend for us and for the drivers. And it's new tracks like Kansas Speedway that will help move NASCAR forward."

The Indy Racing League saw similar excitement. The sold-out race marked the midway point for the eights season of the IRL, the nation's premier open-wheel series.

"Kansas is a beautiful race track," the track's inaugural IRL winner and 1998 Indianapolis 500 winner Eddie Cheever Jr. said. "There was a time when most of the kids who wanted to be IndyCar Series drivers came out of Indianapolis. I wouldn't be surprised if the next generation of drivers came from Kansas City. And it's all because of the beautiful, world-class facility you have."

Cheever said the growth of the IRL and its recent success can be directly attributed to Kansas Speedway.

"You're building a new fan base here in Kansas City, and that helps the growth of our sport," Cheever said.

Two-time Indianapolis 500 winner, Al Unser Jr., mirrored Cheever's statement, adding it was the new fans who helped make Kansas Speedway's Indy Racing League IndyCar Series race weekends great events.

"I met some new fans who had never attended an IRL event before and all they could talk about is how great the race and the race track were," Unser Jr. said. "It's that excitement from the fans that makes me want to come back to Kansas City."

THE TRACK

When Kansas Speedway opened to sold-out crowds in 2001, it was the start of a new era for NASCAR and the IRL. A new era of speedway palaces has cropped up and other tracks are taking notice.

Motorsports have become the No. 1 spectator sport in the county. It has gone from a hobby sport held on beaches and dirt tracks to televised extravaganzas held in $200 million complexes.

With its growing popularity and visibility, the sport is demanding increasingly sophisticated facilities with features and amenities found at other major-league sports venues.

International Speedway Corporation, the company that owns Kansas Speedway, recognized the changing trends in racing and the sport's fabulous potential, especially in the Midwest.

Racing is no longer just a sport for men. Today, nearly half of fans are women and families with children. In response to this ever-increasing diversity, Kansas Speedway incorporated new amenities and features traditionally not found at other speedways.

Kansas Speedway is one of the first tracks ISC had built in nearly 40 years. Trends 40 years ago weren't necessary back then. But today, speedways are competing for a family's entertainment dollar.

Within the track infield, Fan Walk provides a first-of-its-kind area for fans to get close to the action in the garages and pits. In an attempt to bring the race-day experience full circle, Fan Walk allows spectators a clear view of the inspection process prior to the race. Two inspection garages and fueling stations have elevated risers where fans can see every car as it is inspected.

To foster the accessibility drivers have always had with fans, Fan Walk is surrounded by a fence with a horizontal opening to allow fans to hand items to drivers for autographs. The area also has an elevated stage for live entertainment – a place where fans often meet their favorite drivers or watch a press conference.

The traditional metal bleachers, with their lattice of spindly supports, have been replaced at Kansas Speedway by concrete columns and a more simplified seating structure.

The predominant color scheme of blue and gold throughout the speedway was derived from the colors of the Kansas state flag. These colors are woven throughout the concession stands and restrooms, suites, garages, and the icon tower.

The pattern of colors in the grandstand seating is an abstract image of sunflowers with the on-grade green seats in the lower sections representing the rolling hills of Kansas.

"I get excited each time I go to Kansas City," said Helio Castroneves, 2001 and 2002 Indianapolis 500 winner. "Anytime we can go into a community of people who are excited about racing and excited about us being there, it makes for a good event."

So change has not only hit the drivers, paint schemes and technology of the cars. It's hit with the design and development Kansas Speedway, the youngest speedway on the NASCAR circuit.

"There's change everywhere, it just seems like it's hit our sport in a lot bigger lump than it does other sports," said Harvick. "Change is not necessarily bad. It brings a new realm of excitement and I'm glad to be a part of it."

ENOUGH MEMORIES TO GO AROUND

BY RICK PETERSON

THE 2005 RACING SEASON MAY BE NO. 5 FOR KANSAS SPEEDWAY, BUT FANS ALL OVER THE MIDWEST STILL FEEL THE NEED TO PINCH THEMSELVES FROM TIME TO TIME JUST TO REMIND THEMSELVES THAT THEY REALLY DO HAVE A STATE-OF-THE-ART MOTORSPORTS FACILITY SO CLOSE TO THEIR HOMES AND HEARTS.

"We rubber-necked against the fence watching the drivers and their cars go by and just the rumble of the cars.
You just felt it all over."

"It was wonderful to get something that close, too close to where you just can't not go," said Lynda Bell of Kansas City, MO. "I just love drinking a cup of coffee and watching the sun come up over the track at 6 o'clock in the morning."

"I never thought that it would come to fruition," Keith Hughes, Olathe, KS, said. "I've really enjoyed the time that I've been able to spend with my dad and everything else out there. The highlight for me is probably just the overall enjoyment and how the sport itself as grown."

"I think it's just a neat place to go and watch a race," Ron Lane, Marion, IA, said.

Once it was a fact that Kansas Speedway was going to happen, fans from all over the Midwest flocked to get tickets.

"We put our money down when it was still dirt," said Linda Schoor of Belton, MO.

In 2001, when the track finally opened , fans knew that the long wait had been well worth it.

"What I remember is the first year when you were actually seeing a Cup race in person for the first time and to watch 43 drivers come around and just watch that green flag fly and the race is on and you're actually watching it," Schoor said. "That's probably the most exciting thing and the one that sticks out clearer of any of the races. Watching them on TV is one thing, seeing it in person is another – that very first race."

For Schoor and Vicky Ford of Raymore, MO, just getting within shouting distance of their beloved drivers was a thrill in itself.

"The Fan Walk that they put here is just incredible, for the fans to have such great access," Ford said.

Schoor agreed.

"We rubber-necked against the fence watching the drivers and their cars

go by and just the rumble of the cars. You just felt it all over," she said. "To me that was a very exciting thing, being that close to them."

If you talk to 100 fans you're likely to hear 100 different fondest memories and, even though it's only been four short seasons, there's plenty to go around.

For some, the No. 1 memory is Jeff Gordon's victory – the first of his two straight Kansas wins – in the Speedway's first NASCAR NEXTEL (then Winston) Cup race on Sept. 30, 2001.

There are other fans who lean towards the late Ricky Hendrick winning the Speedway's inaugural NASCAR Craftsman Truck Series race on July 7, 2001, his biggest win before dying tragically in a plane crash on Oct. 24, 2004.

As far as pure on-track racing excitement, it's hard to top Buddy Rice's July 4, 2004 win by five-thousandths of a second over Vitor Meira in the Indy Racing League's Argent Mortgage 300.

And no driver in any series has dominated Kansas Speedway like Joe Nemechek dominated it Oct. 2004, winning the NEXTEL Cup pole, the Busch Series event and the NEXTEL Cup race in a span of about 48 hours.

But some figure that their fondest Kansas Speedway memory could be just around the corner.

"It just gets better and better," Ford said.

THE FANS' FANTASTIC FIVE

1. JEFF GORDON WINS INAUGURAL CUP EVENT

One of auto racing's biggest names won the biggest race in Kansas history, winning by 0.413 of a second over Ryan Newman to leave Gordon fans ecstatic.

"I'm one of those kind of Gordon fans that, even though I like Hendrick Motorsports and I like Jimmie Johnson and I try my hardest to root for them, once something happens to Gordon in a NASCAR race my level of enthusiasm for the race goes down at least 50 percent. I try my hardest to still get into it, but once he falls out of the race, I just watch it.

"It actually took me three years to get those tickets. I put my name in the hat before they broke ground, the whole nine yards, and it was just year after year that I waited. And then to go to the first race and for him to win it, that was like the track came full circle for me. The whole effort seemed to be worth it." — John Hirsch, Beggs, OK.

2. BUDDY RICE BY AN EYELASH

A little over a month after winning the Indianapolis 500, Rice prevailed at Kansas Speedway by 0.0051 of a second over Vitor Meira, ending a 10-lap battle at the end of the July 4, 2004 race, which ranked as the second-closest finish in Indy Racing League history.

"It was just really exciting to be able to watch that here in my home state. It was quite a thrill. It was so close. There's so many IndyCar races like that anymore that are so close and you sort of have to wait and see to make sure who won. There are so many that come down to the last lap, the last turn."
— Larry Larson, Wichita, KS.

3. FRONT ROW JOE TIMES THREE

Joe Nemechek came to Kansas Speedway in October, sitting 24th in NEXTEL Cup points and fighting a long victory drought. He left with Busch Series and NEXTEL Cup wins as well as a Cup pole, upstaging the 10 Chase for the Championship competitors.

"A lot of the big names have won there, but it also sticks out that some of the not-so-big names have won there, too. Look at Joe Nemechek. He swept the whole weekend – the pole on Friday, Busch on Saturday and Cup on Sunday. That's never happened at our track – that was the first time. Coming up here and pulling off that feat is amazing. He kind of put a spoiler on things, too, because the race this year was the fourth one in the Chase for the Cup and he was kind of a spoiler because he wasn't in that Chase."
— Lynda Bell, Kansas City, MO.

4. RICKY HENDRICK WINS TRUCK EVENT

The son of famed NASCAR owner Rick Hendrick found the winner's circle for his first major victory, with the 21-year-old winning the July 7, 2001 NASCAR Craftsman Truck Series event by 2.841 seconds over Ted Musgrave. Hendrick's victory took on added meaning for racing fans on Oct. 24, 2004 when Hendrick died in a plane crash en route to Martinsville, VA, at the age of 24.

"That (Hendrick's victory) was pretty neat and now it has a little more significance with what happened." — Ron Lane, Marion, IA.

"Wins are nice, but when you see your son do something it's really special and very emotional. You think about when he was sitting in your lap or in (Ken) Schrader's lap. He's kind of like the mascot to a football team that ended up being the quarterback." — Rick Hendrick, July 7, 2001.

5. REMEMBERING FALLEN AMERICAN HEROES

The timing of Kansas Speedway's inaugural NASCAR Cup race in 2001 was bittersweet for race fans for a couple of reasons.

There was a huge throng of Dale Earnhardt fans who had been looking forward to seeing their hero race in Kansas. That dream ended when Earnhardt was killed in the Daytona 500 in February of that year. Fans honored Earnhardt and his legendary No. 3 car on the third lap of the first event.

"I remember vividly getting my tickets for Christmas from my wife. My favorite driver was Dale Earnhardt. I couldn't wait to see him in person. Then Daytona happened and, well, that brought out a whole different feel to the NASCAR race that year. I remember the silence of the crowd and the hand signals of three that the fans participated in all that season of NASCAR. It was certainly different than on TV." — Corey Wilson, Topeka, KS.

The inaugural Cup race was also bittersweet because it came just a little over two weeks following the Sept. 11, 2001 tragedy that rocked the nation.

"They handed our red, white and blue flags and people waved them when the race started and of course on the third lap everybody was raising their hand for No. 3 for Earnhardt. That was a pretty memorable year." — Ron Lane, Marion, IA.

"The one thing that always stood out for me was the security after 9-11. We always talk about that, how the helicopters were flying over with the gun turrets hanging out. Nobody knew exactly what was going to happen, but they were wanting you to be safe." — Keith Hughes, Olathe, KS.

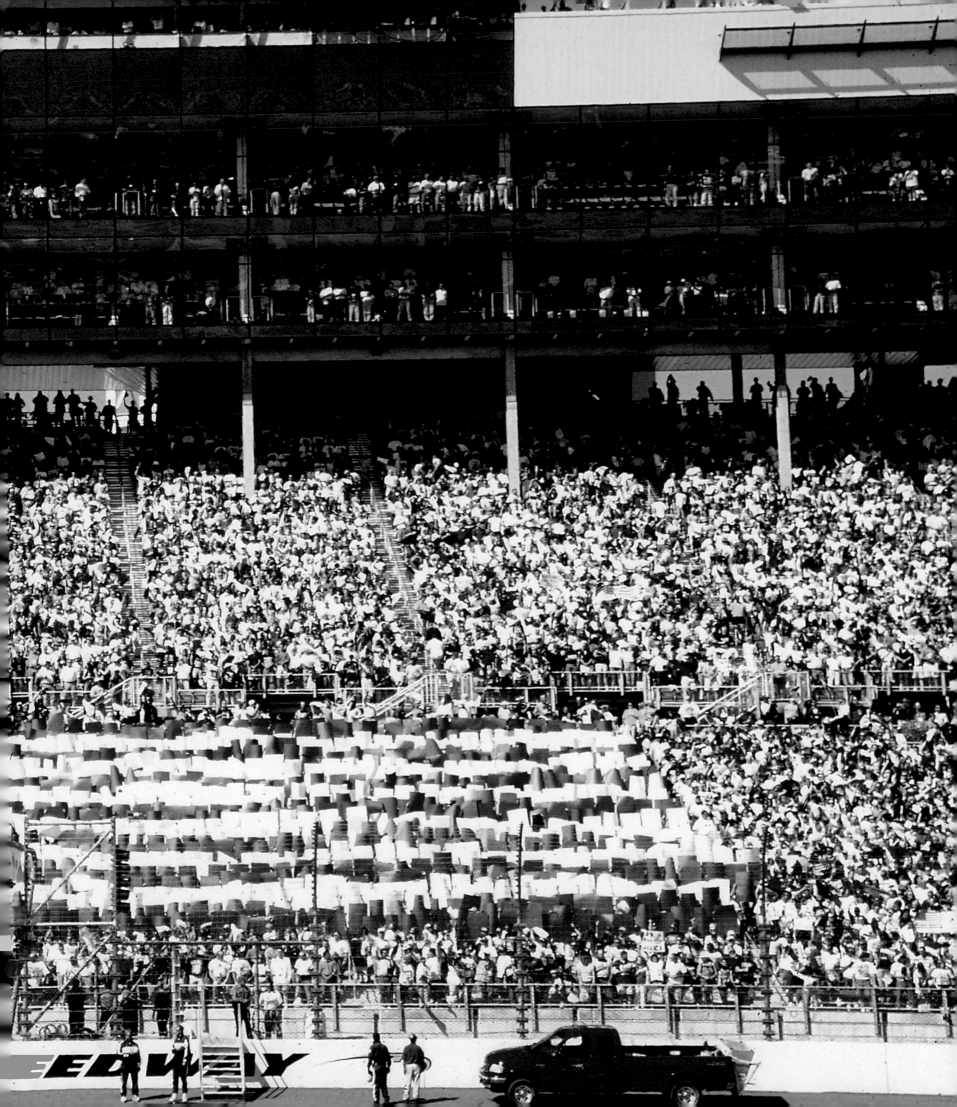

A MARGIN OF VICTORY

BY CURT CAVIN

BUDDY RICE GLANCED TO HIS RIGHT AS HE HAD DONE SO MANY TIMES THAT JULY DAY AT KANSAS SPEEDWAY IN 2004. THE OBJECT IN HIS MIRROR WAS INDEED LARGER THAN HE HAD HOPED. FELLOW INDY RACING LEAGUE DRIVER VITOR MEIRA HAD ALL BUT ATTACHED HIS RACE CAR TO RICE'S SIDE, AND HE WAS SHOWING NO SIGNS OF BACKING OFF.

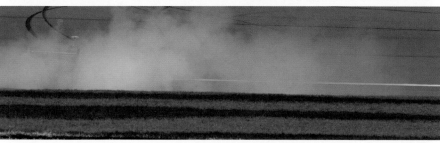

Rice knew he couldn't push his accelerator pedal any closer to the floor, so he clutched his steering wheel a little tighter, checked his patience and rode around the sweeping track as best he could.

The side-by-side duel in the Argent Mortgage Indy 300 continued for the final 30 laps of the race. Inches apart at 210 mph, Rice, the reigning Indianapolis 500 winner, and Meira, his upstart teammate at Rahal Letterman Racing, battled all the way to the finish line, separated by little more than a blink of an eye as the checkered flag waved.

Officially, the computer clock showed Rice won by 0.0051 seconds, a distance of about 18 inches. Bobby Rahal, the former IndyCar champion who shared ownership in both cars, couldn't discern a winner from his pit-road position 100 yards away.

"I'd have guessed Vitor won," he said.

Conceded Rice: "Me, too."

Rice's margin of victory ended up being the narrowest in major auto racing for the 2004 season, and it was the second-closest in the IRL's nine seasons of action. But the separation didn't come as a surprise to those who have been watching the transformation of Indy-car racing. In fact, it was more of the same.

Since 1.5-mile tracks like Kansas Speedway have been built, the IRL has consistently produced thrilling finishes. Forty-four of the first 100 races in league history had a margin of victory less than one second. Half of those came at tracks similar in design to Kansas, which has had three such thrilling finishes.

In the inaugural IRL race at Kansas in 2001, Eddie Cheever Jr. edged Sam Hornish Jr. by 0.1976 seconds. Hornish also was on the losing end of a 0.1741-second battle in 2002. That day's winner was Airton Dare.

The other tracks of such configuration are Atlanta Motor Speedway, Texas Motor Speedway in Fort Worth, Las Vegas Motor Speedway, Chicagoland Speedway in Joliet, IL, and Kentucky Speedway in Sparta, KY. Homestead-Miami (FL) Speedway joined the group in 2003 when its pavement was torn up and its banking in the corners significantly increased.

Each of those tracks has corner banking of at least 14 degrees, and some are as steep as 24 degrees. Each of those tracks has a wide and fast racing line, permitting speeds that reached 226 mph in 1998 before IRL officials implemented changes to slow the cars down for safety reasons.

"Racy joints," former driver Scott Goodyear said of the 1.5-mile tracks. "They definitely make you think about (retirement), but they're what made the IRL what it is today."

The ability to race close is keyed by wing designs that uses flowing air to plant the cars to the track, a phenomenon known as downforce. Downforce

is the opposite of lift created by the wings of an airplane during takeoff.

The flow of air over the top of a car creates a trailing vacuum, called the draft, that allows chasing drivers to gain speed as they close in on a competitor. An IndyCar driver can feel the draft from more than 100 yards away, allowing their cars to bunch together and create close racing.

The closest finish in IRL history was Hornish's 0.0024-second victory over Al Unser Jr. at Chicagoland in 2002. Hornish instinctively raised his right arm at the checkered flag, but he later admitted it was too close for him to call.

Chicagoland also had the fourth-closest finish in IRL history with Hornish's 0.0099-second victory over Scott Dixon in 2003. That race also stands as the closest 1-2-3 finish in league history with third-place finisher Bryan Herta virtually side-by-side with Hornish and Dixon. In fact, all five of the league's closest 1-2-3 finishes came on 1.5-mile tracks, with Hornish winning four of them.

Not surprisingly, three of the 1.5-mile tracks (Kentucky, Atlanta and Chicagoland) have produced the three closest qualifying sessions in IRL history as drivers plant their right foot on the gas and steer.

Texas delivered its closest ending (No. 3 all-time) when Hornish nipped Helio Castroneves by 0.0096 seconds in 2003. Homestead, Las Vegas and Atlanta all have had finishes that are among the sport's top 20.

Get the idea?

"There's just something magical that happens when you get our cars on those kinds of tracks," said Unser, who also lost a close one to Jeff Ward at Texas (0.0111 seconds in 2002) before holding off Tony Kanaan on the same track a year later (by 0.0810 seconds). "It's definitely what makes the IRL stand out. People love to watch the shootouts."

Other forms of racing are envious of the IRL's thrillers. With 36 opportunities in 2004, NASCAR's Nextel Cup division had only three races post margins of victory less than one second, one of them at Kansas. The Champ Car World Series, which is the IRL's counterpart in American open-wheel racing, had only one such close finish, and that came at Las Vegas with a wing package similar to the IRL's.

Forget Formula One producing memorable and close finishes. Michael Schumacher's Ferrari often laps the field.

IndyCar racing hasn't always raced this close, however. Prior to Tony George's creation of the IRL in 1996, the closest finish in Indy-car history was Unser's 0.043-second victory over Goodyear in the 1992 Indianapolis 500. Today, that margin wouldn't break the IRL's top 20.

The first 50 years of the Indy 500 saw only two drivers win by fewer than 10 seconds. Jules Goux won the 1913 race by more than 13 minutes. As late as 1972, Mark Donohue won by more than three minutes.

Today, fans love close finishes. Deep down, it's the drivers who are nervous.

Robby McGehee broke his leg in 2001 when his car got tangled in a three-car fight for the lead late in a race at Texas. On the same track three years later, Kenny Brack flipped into the fence after making tire contact with Tomas Scheckter.

Every shootout is a hospital visit begging to be arranged, but the drivers know the risk and accept it.

"Part of the game, unfortunately," said Kanaan, who broke his wrist in a late-race crash fighting for the lead at the Twin Ring Motegi track in Japan in 2003. "We race close and sometimes things happen. No one likes to see it, but it's part of what happens on these tracks. NASCAR has Daytona and Talladega; we have the mile-and-a-half tracks."

CONTROLLED MADNESS

As a publicist of the half-mile Bristol (TN) Motor Speedway and a longtime NASCAR follower, Wayne Estes attended one of the IRL's early races at Texas Motor Speedway in 1998.

Twenty-eight cars started the race in two-by-two formation. For the better part of an hour, through a green-flag pit stop and over half of the 208 laps, the front half of the field ran in a pack, too close for comfort at speeds approaching 225 mph.

"You couldn't put your hand between the tires of the cars," Eddie Cheever said. "As a driver, you just held your breath and held on, hoping someone wouldn't make a mistake."

The tension mounted with each lap, and almost no one in the crowd of 80,000 people sat down. Estes, who had only watched the IRL on television, finally decided he was exhausted by the live version.

"This," he said after an exhale, "is unnecessary."

That type of response still draws a chuckle from Brian Barnhart, a former IRL mechanic who is now the league's president. He knows that close racing is the hallmark of the league on oval tracks.

"I challenge anyone to find better racing than what we've got," he said.

"You couldn't put your hand between the tires of the cars. As a driver, you just held your breath and held on, hoping someone wouldn't make a mistake."

— Eddie Cheever

While the IRL's attendance figures and television ratings have not grown as NASCAR's have, there's no questioning the league's on-track product, particularly on the 1.5-mile tracks. When the IRL raced at similarly configured Lowe's Motor Speedway in Concord, NC, for the first time in 1997, a handful of curious NASCAR competitors showed up for a look-see. Word got out. The next year, the IRL's paddock was a Who's Who of the stock-car world.

"If you're a race fan, you had to see this," Ray Evernham said that weekend.

That race didn't even have a close finish. Buddy Lazier won by 3.3 seconds, which would have been the second-largest spread had it been posted during the 2004 season.

While Sam Hornish Jr. has won an IRL-best eight races on 1.5-mile tracks, he is by no means able to control the action. The fall race he won at Texas in 2001 saw 32 lead changes, the second-most in league history. The IRL averaged 15.3 lead changes on 1.5-mile tracks in 2004, with Kansas having 18 as Buddy Rice and Vitor Meira surged back and forth in their side-by-side pursuit.

Conversely, none of the races on the "fewest lead changes" list were held on 1.5-mile tracks.

"There's too much going on out there for one guy to dominate," Kanaan said. "Can't happen."

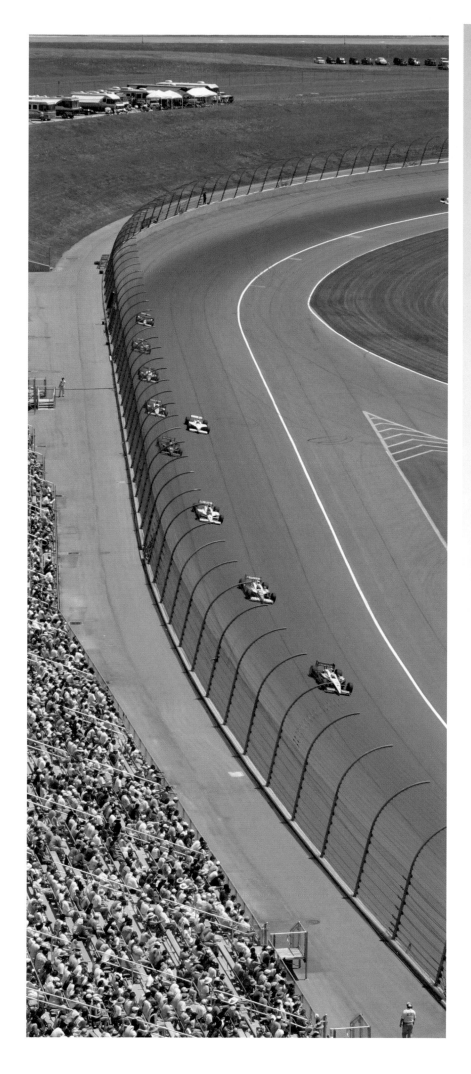

FELIPE GIAFFONE

Auto racing sometimes plays cruel games on its participants.

In July of 2003, Felipe Giaffone, a former Rookie of the Year at the Indianapolis 500, was driving for one of the Indy Racing League's better teams. He was coming off a season that included his first career victory.

Battling in the lead pack at Kansas Speedway, his car was struck in the left rear. Suddenly, everything in Giaffone's life began spinning.

The car hit the outside wall with terrific force, breaking the upper portion of Giaffone's leg and his pelvis. The Brazilian spent the next six weeks recovering from the injuries.

While Giaffone returned to compete later in the season, more struggles would follow. His sponsor left him at the end of the year, preventing his return to the team the next season.

Giaffone doesn't hold a grudge on the competitor who initiated the contact nor does the track give him bad vibes when he returns.

"I just remember that I wanted someone to hit me in the head with a hammer (after the accident) because I was awake the whole time," he said. "Things like this happen in racing. It happened. We move on."

"Still, the IRL's success on the high banks boils down to the level of confidence and car control a driver possesses. One misstep can send cars ricocheting into one another..."

The four IRL races at Kansas have been won by four different drivers: Cheever, Airton Dare, Bryan Herta and Rice. There has never been fewer than 10 lead changes, and the pole in qualifying has been won by four different drivers (Scott Sharp, Tomas Scheckter, Scott Dixon and Rice).

In other words, competition rules at Kansas, and it's like that on all of the 1.5-mile tracks.

"It's easy to drive one of these tracks by yourself, but it takes a lot to separate yourself in traffic," Rice said. "That part is tough."

Amazingly, some of the IRL's best overall driving performances have been at Kentucky, Chicagoland and Kansas, tracks that have had three cautions or fewer in a single race. Kentucky's 2003 race had only one yellow flag, and that was for a fire on board Kenny Brack's car.

"There's a lot going on, but we seem to take care of each other on those tracks," Kanaan said. "Guys try to give each other plenty of room, although it might not always seem like that."

Brian Barnhart has made driver-to-driver protection a point of emphasis since he became the IRL's race director in 1997. Two of the harshest penalties he's handed out have been for aggressive driving on 1.5-mile tracks (both at Texas).

It helps "the show" that the 1.5-mile tracks are some of the nicest facilities in the world. Texas and Kansas consistently rank among the best regardless of track size; Texas for its massive seating capacity (about 200,000) and uniform construction, Kansas for its overall layout and amenities.

Kentucky's track is quaintly dug in the side of a Bluegrass hill in the most scenic part of the state. Chicagoland is a poor man's version of Kansas, with a drag strip and a short track at its side to give race fans complete entertainment. The increased banking at Homestead (now 20 degrees in the corners) has improved the quality of the racing for both the IRL and NASCAR.

Still, the IRL's success on the high banks boils down to the level of confidence and car control a driver possesses. One misstep can send cars ricocheting into one another as 11 did in the back of the pack at Atlanta in 2001.

Other than the late-race Texas crash in 2001 that collected Cheever, Robby McGehee and Greg Ray, the IRL has had very few crashes at the 1.5-mile tracks that involve more than two cars.

Drivers hold their respective lines, look for the calm air in the draft, move to the outside line and make passes. Sometimes they ride along side-by-side as Rice and Meira did in 2004 at Kansas.

All the while, fans stand and cheer, car owners hold their collective breath and newcomers such as Bristol's Estes wish the high-speed madness wasn't so maddening.

But at 1.5-mile tracks such as Kansas, Texas, Chicagoland and Kentucky, to name a few, that's what controlled madness looks like.

SPEEDWAY VICTORIES: DIVERSITY IS THE NAME OF THE GAME

BY CURT CAVIN

KANSAS SPEEDWAY HAS HAD A LITTLE BIT OF EVERYTHING IN ITS FIRST FOUR INDY RACING LEAGUE RACE WINNERS. TWO DRIVERS DEFINED THEIR CAREERS WITH INDIANAPOLIS 500 VICTORIES. ANOTHER DRIVER WON THE FIRST INDYCAR RACE OF HIS CAREER AT THE TRACK WHILE THE FOURTH WAS KNOWN MORE FOR HIS ROAD RACING SKILLS.

Eddie Cheever Jr. won his final IRL race at Kansas; Airton Dare and Bryan Herta won their first. None of them finished in the season's top five. Herta's victory was his first on an oval track.

Only Buddy Rice, the Indy 500 winner in 2004, sustained his season's momentum to Kansas, at Kansas and through Kansas. His victory on July 4, 2004, was part of a season that saw him win three races and finish third in the standings.

"It's just a track that can be unpredictable with the way (the IndyCars) race there," said 2004 IRL champion Tony Kanaan. "It's a tough place to race."

Cheever, the 1998 Indy winner, won his Kansas race in the track's inaugural 2001 season. It also was one of only three IRL victories in six seasons for the Infiniti engine.

Dare won in 2002 as part of a double-victory weekend for team owner A.J. Foyt, whose grandson, A.J. IV, won the IRL's first Pro Series race. Dare, a Brazilian, came from the sixth starting spot to win that race, but he

essentially came from nowhere. In 38 career starts, he led only six races for 37 laps. Eight of those laps came that day at Kansas.

Herta was even more of a surprise winner. The race was just his third in the IRL, and he was substituting for the injured Dario Franchitti who had surgery on his back following a motorcycle accident in April. Herta's only two victories in the Champ Car World Series were at the Laguna Seca road course in Monterey, CA (1998 and 1999, both from the pole). Herta won Kansas because his team gambled on fuel strategy and prevailed.

Rice's victory at Kansas surprised no one. He had dominated Indy, leading 91 of the 160 laps, and the pole he won at Kansas was his third in seven races. He would win additional poles at Nashville and Kentucky and another race at Michigan.

At Kansas, Rice led 83 of the 200 laps, but his drive to victory lane wasn't that straightforward. He had to hold off a charging Vitor Meira, his teammate at Rahal Letterman Racing, prevailing by 0.0051 seconds at the checkered flag, the second-closest finish in IRL history.

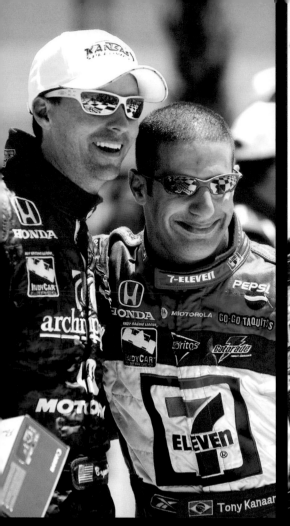

Meira deserved to be the winner and another first-time winner for an IRL driver at Kansas. He led 37 laps and was easily the fastest driver of the day. Pit road problems twice cost him track position, forcing him to come scrambling back through the field to challenge Rice.

The Kansas race winners are as diverse as the league provides.

Cheever represented the league's old guard when he won the race at age 43. Born in Phoenix, he was raised in Rome, becoming one of the most successful U.S.-born Formula One drivers in history. His 132 starts in the series from 1978 to 1989 remains more than any American driver.

Cheever returned to the States in 1990, winning Rookie of the Year honors at Indy with Ganassi Racing. In 1996, Cheever recorded 22 of the fastest 50 laps of the 500, including an all-time race record lap of 236.103 mph.

When Cheever won Indy in 1998, he drove for himself in a car that wasn't among the most funded in the field. He started 17th in a car sponsored by Rachel's Gourmet Potato Chips. Rachel's has long since faded from most people's memories.

There are many more familiar Brazilian IndyCar drivers than Dare. Chief among them are former Indy 500 winners Emerson Fittipaldi, Helio Castroneves and Gil de Ferran.

Dare reached the IRL in 2000 and won Rookie-of-the-Year honors with since-defunct Team Xtreme, a Dallas-based operation. He was 24 years old when he won at Kansas, but his IndyCar career ended in 2003 when he crashed hard in practice at Texas Motor Speedway, a month before trying to defend his Kansas victory.

Herta, who in 2005 is competing in his third IRL season, was out of place when he joined Andretti Green Racing as Franchitti's replacement in 2003. He had spent at least part of nine seasons in Champ Car, but he landed the part-time job because of his friendship with team co-owner Michael Andretti, who won Champ Car's title in 1991.

Even though Herta has long been considered one of the nation's top road racers, his career has never seemed to reach its potential. He won the Indy Lights championship in 1993, but he suffered season-ending leg and pelvis during a crash in practice at Toronto the next year.

Never finishing higher than eighth in the standings, Herta frequently bounced around between teams. In 2000 he was Champ Car's super sub, filling in at Mo Nunn Racing for the injured Kanaan and at Walker Racing for the injured Shinji Nakano. Herta finished fifth at Long Beach for Walker, which held as his season's best drive until he finished fourth for Forsythe Racing at Laguna Seca.

But by 2002, there wasn't a Champ Car ride for him. He joined the Panoz factory team to compete in the American LeMans Series and might have remained there had Andretti not called.

Herta's 2003 season was defined by the victory at Kansas, but he had five other top-five finishes in 11 races, including a string of thirds at Kentucky, Nazareth and Chicagoland. That consistency earned the native of Valencia, Calif., a full-time ride with Andretti Green, which expanded to its current four-car lineup.

Like Cheever, Rice was born in Phoenix. But unlike Cheever, Rice never left the Valley of the Sun.

Having watched him win the Indy 500 in 2004, it's easy to consider Rice, the Toyota Atlantic series champion in 2000, a life-long frontrunner. But he went rideless in 2001 and was only a part-timer for Cheever Racing in 2002.

The 2003 season wasn't the best for Rice, either. When the Chevrolet engine couldn't compete with IRL newcomers Toyota and Honda, Rice was deemed part of the problem. After failing to finish higher than ninth in any of the first 13 races of the season, Rice was released in favor of Alex Barron.

Bobby Rahal didn't pass on the chance to claim the 28-year-old Rice, who would serve as the replacement for the injured Kenny Bräck. Rice never left the team because Bräck didn't return – and the rest is history.

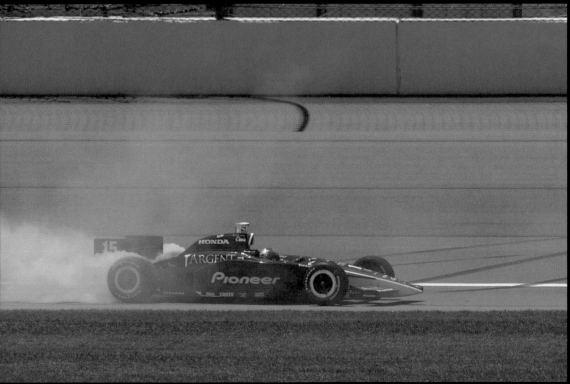

PAVING THE WAY

by **DAVID CONRADS** photography by **GARY ROHMAN**

KANSAS CITY, KANSAS AND WYANDOTTE COUNTY HAVE BEEN ON A PROMINENT UPSWING IN FORTUNES FOR THE PAST SEVERAL YEARS. AFTER DECADES OF STEADY POPULATION AND RETAIL BUSINESS DECLINE, THE OPENING OF KANSAS SPEEDWAY IN 2001 ACTED AS A CATALYST FOR INCREDIBLE NEW BUSINESS AND POPULATION GROWTH.

The numbers continue to rise with new businesses, new restaurants, new attractions, real estate tax revenues, new housing starts, tourism dollars and overnight hotel stays as an economic development boom continues in Wyandotte County. The growth is so incredible that years from now, when the history of the metropolitan Kansas City area is written, the opening of Kansas Speedway may stand as the starting point of an economic boon era not only for Wyandotte County but the region as well.

The Unified Government of Wyandotte County/Kansas City, Kansas purchased a 400-acre tract of mostly agricultural land adjacent to Kansas Speedway as part of a planned tourism district, now known as Village West. Using state and legislatively approved economic development tools, the once rural area is now filled with customers at Cabela's an outdoor outfitter; Nebraska Furniture Mart; The Great Wolf Lodge, which includes a 37,000 sq. ft. indoor water park; Community America Ballpark, home of the Kansas City T-Bones; and many other shopping, dining and entertainment possibilities.

Not only are these entities attracting the customers, but the Village West's return on investment currently includes over $5 million annually in property taxes to the district along with several thousand jobs, both full and part-time.

New development is also taking place just outside the original 400 acres with both commercial building as well as record breaking new housing starts throughout the Northwestern part of the city.

"It's succeeding way beyond our loftiest expectations," said Jim Thompson, president/CEO of Wyandotte Development, Inc., a county-wide public/private economic development organization that fosters and assists new and existing businesses in the county. Wyandotte Development was one of the many public and private entities that worked together to convince International Speedway Corporation (ISC) to build the 1.5-mile oval state-of-the-art track in Kansas City, Kansas.

Cindy Cash, president/CEO of the Kansas City Kansas Area Chamber of Commerce, agrees Kansas Speedway and Village West are responsible for an incredible turn around for the county, but she also points out the partnership that helped make Kansas Speedway, and subsequently Village West, a reality.

"There was an incredible group of people working on this. The Unified Government of Wyandotte County/Kansas City, Kansas, led by then Mayor Carol Marinovich, the Unified Government Commissioners, along with a very talented staff, were certainly drivers of the process. The State of Kansas was very involved, from the Governor, Lt. Governor, Department of Commerce, state representatives and senators, the Board of Public Utilities, citizens

from all walks of life, Wyandotte Development, the KCK Chamber, Kansas City Area Development Council and the regional economic development organization. A very talented marketing agency created a video "Our Hearts Are Racing" which truly showed why our community wanted Kansas Speedway here. Another piece that helped sell the idea was an ad placed in the Daytona papers the morning of the Kansas City, Kansas presentation from surrounding Kansas cities, chambers and economic development organizations that supported our bid for the speedway."

However, not everyone in the community was keen on the idea during the early stages in the late 90s. Like any project of such magnitude, Kansas Speedway and Village West had its share of opposition and controversy. For one thing, four businesses and 146 homeowners, some of whom had lived on their property for generations, had to be relocated. This was not an easy decision for Unified Government elected officials to make, nor the affected businesses and homeowners to accept.

There was also the financial consideration of a 30-year property tax abatement that was given to ISC for Kansas Speedway. Although there was a dedicated group of racing fans in the area who had enjoyed attending at nearby Lakeside Speedway – a dirt track – many Wyandotte County residents were suspicious of what seemed like a corporate give away and

wondered if this massive upheaval and tax abatement would really pay off for this struggling community.

As soon as the first bids were opened for the building of Kansas Speedway, a positive impact was felt, first throughout the construction industry. Then, as Kansas Speedway prepared for its first season, local vendors were needed to supplement the food needs of the catering company Americrown, as well as other needs such as paper goods, cleaning services, signage, and other supplies.

On race days, the workforce population at Kansas Speedway swells to the size of a small city, with both paid and volunteer workers. Non-profit organizations are solicited by Kansas Speedway to work certain areas on race days for a share of income or an honorarium back to the non-profit.

"Kansas Speedway and the development that has occurred around the area have changed many things," said Steve Kelly, deputy secretary of the Kansas Department of Commerce. "But the thing that can't be overemphasized is the change in attitude and the idea that we can get things done. We've shown that we can be successful on a major project that was very complicated and very difficult to do, that was not unanimously supported at first and had opposition from a number of different sources. But by sticking with it and working together, we were able to get it done and it has shown itself to be not only what we envisioned, but maybe more than what we ever thought."

"I grew up and live in the Piper area, the area where Kansas Speedway and Village West now sits," said Bridgette Jobe, director of the Kansas City, Kansas/Wyandotte County Convention and Visitors Bureau. When I was growing up, the area was farmland. Now we are the center of activity. We've changed from a rural community to the center of tourism for the state."

Since the opening of Kansas Speedway and Village West, the CVB's work has not only grown by leaps and bounds, but it has changed drastically.

"Prior to the opening of Kansas Speedway and Village West, we had some wonderful historic sites and museums, great parks and an active music amphitheater. But we were not a tourism destination; now we are," continued Ms. Jobe. "When I tell people I work in tourism in Wyandotte County, people tell me I must have the best job in the world!"

Now Jobe's work includes marketing not only Kansas Speedway, but also Village West and the other original attractions Kansas City, Kansas/Wyandotte County offers.

"Now we are attractive to the motor coach operators. We can keep people busy for two to three days. We are so centrally located that we appeal to many families looking for a weekend get away and keep kids from 1 – 90 entertained."

The work at the CVB has become challenging. "It's more a matter of which leisure travel group do we concentrate our efforts on," continues Jobe, "This year, we're focusing on Des Moines and piggybacking on some other efforts. Our impact studies show that 63 percent of our visitors come from outside of Kansas and Missouri."

The building of Kansas Speedway and Village West in the greenfield western part of the county is beginning to pay off in other parts of the community as well. Housing has grown by leaps and bounds in the area north and west of the new development. "We have had five years of record breaking new housing starts after many years of with little activity." said Thompson. Three miles to the east of Kansas Speedway, the first Lowe's Home Improvement store opened in Wyandotte County. The western development has also spurred new interest in reviving a dated and in many areas blighted eastern part of the county."

"The success out west has proven this community can make things happen," said Cash, "Developers are interested in helping re-develop other parts of our community, Kansas Speedway has certainly paved the way to make many things happen in our community."

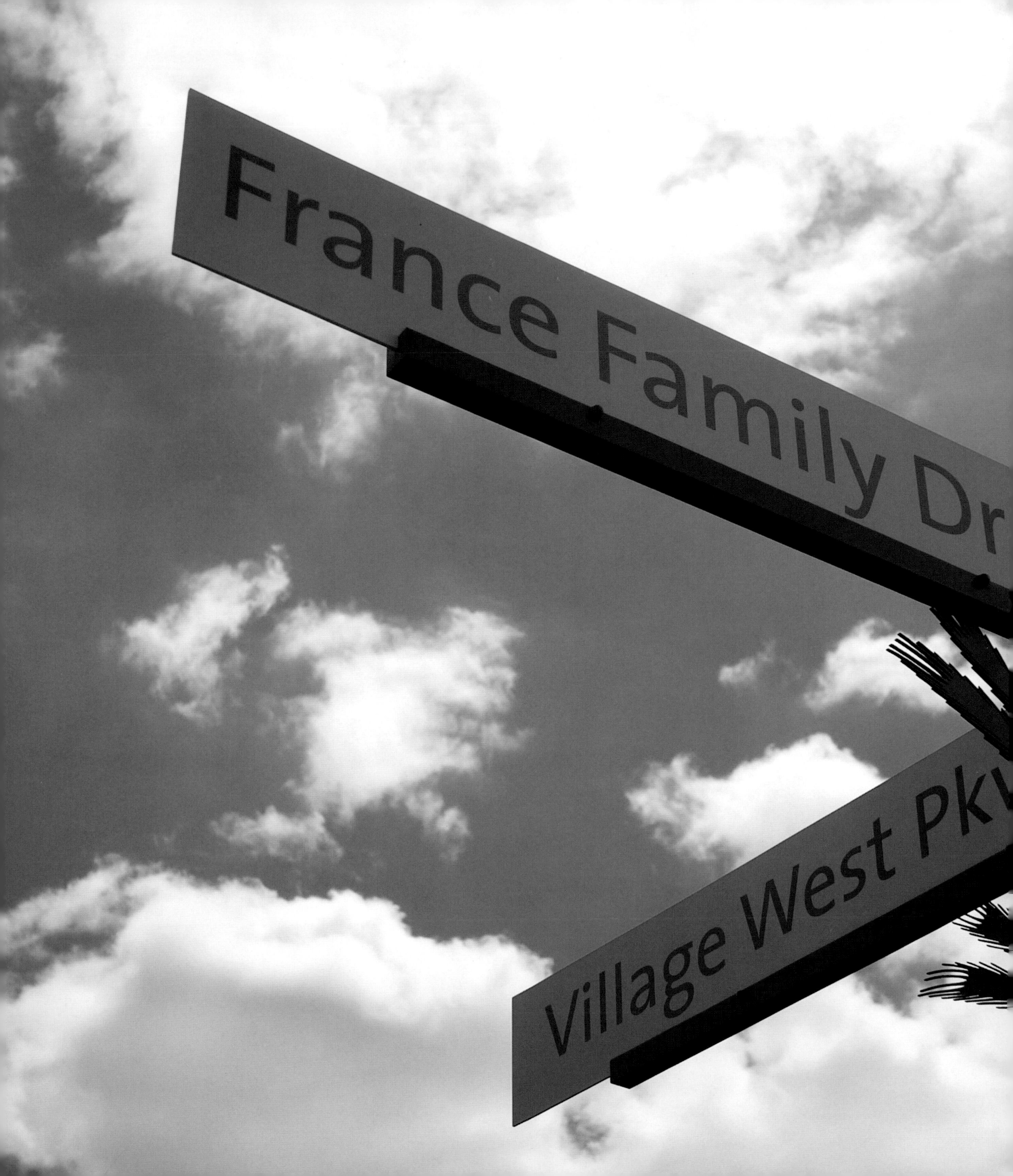
France Family Dr
Village West Pkw

IT TAKES A
TEAM
TO BUILD A
RACETRACK

by DAVID CONRADS
photography by GARY ROHMAN

WITHOUT A DOUBT, KANSAS SPEEDWAY HAS BEEN THE BIGGEST BOOST TO THE ECONOMY OF WYANDOTTE COUNTY IN A GENERATION. AND IT'S PROBABLY NO EXAGGERATION TO CLAIM THE SPEEDWAY AND VILLAGE WEST, THE ADJACENT TOURISM DISTRICT, AS THE JEWEL IN THE CROWN OF ECONOMIC AND TOURISM DEVELOPMENT FOR THE ENTIRE STATE OF KANSAS. IN TERMS OF DOLLARS, AMENITIES, JOBS AND PRESTIGE, THE CONTRIBUTION KANSAS SPEEDWAY HAS MADE TO THE BETTERMENT OF THE COUNTY AND THE STATE IS DIFFICULT TO OVERESTIMATE.

A project of this scale does not come about without an extraordinary effort. Convincing the International Speedway Corporation (ISC) to locate a new race track in Wyandotte County was the result of efforts by innumerable public organizations, civic groups, corporations and private citizens – truly a team effort from beginning to end.

Leading the charge was, first, the city council of Kansas City, KS, and then the newly formed Unified Government of Wyandotte County and Kansas City, KS. The late 1990s was a busy time in local government offices, as one of the area's biggest economic development projects coincided with the combining of the city and county governments. April 1, 1997, was a particularly historic day. On that day county residents went to the poles to vote on consolidation while the team representing the county met with the ISC in Daytona to declare its intent to submit a proposal to bring a new race track to Wyandotte County.

Prior to this, a group of local officials traveled to Fontana, CA, to attend the opening of California Speedway and to meet with their counterparts in Fontana to get insight into that community's experience with hosting the ISC. Although none of the team that traveled to Fontana had ever witnessed a major motorsports event, everyone came away impressed with the family atmosphere that prevailed at California Speedway and convinced that a similar facility would be a great asset to Wyandotte County.

They were also impressed by the potential for publicity, national recognition and a boost to the local economy offered by big-league NASCAR auto racing. "Hosting a Winston Cup (now NEXTEL Cup) race carries the same prestige and excitement as hosting the Super Bowl," Mayor Carol Marinovich declared enthusiastically.

After the Fontana trip, the full Kansas City, KS city council debated the proposal and made the decision to continue to explore the feasibility of bringing a race track to the area. Bill Graves, then-governor of Kansas, was approached to determine the state's interest in the project and a very successful partnership was formed. The state passed the necessary legislation, which allowed the use of revenue bonds and gave a 30-year property tax abatement to the project.

A small, but important component of the package that was presented to the ISC was a short video. Titled "Our Hearts are Racing," the video was made up entirely of Wyandotte County residents talking about their community, what it stands for and the people who make it a special place. It was brief, from the heart and later won a national award. It also contributed in a big way to winning over the International Speedway Corporation. In the words of one ISC official, the entire proposal that was submitted "blew us away!"

Talk to anyone about the efforts to bring the speedway to Kansas City and, without fail, everyone emphasizes the team effort. But a number of individuals made particularly critical contributions, starting with Carol Marinovich, mayor of Kansas City, KS, then mayor/CEO of the Unified Government. "She's truly been the leader in this whole development," says Cindy Cash, president and CEO of the Kansas City Kansas Area Chamber of Commerce.

"She was the driving force," adds Don Denney, spokesman for the Unified Government, who was actively involved in all phases of the speedway project. "She was the glue that held it all together."

Building consensus has always been one of the mayor's strengths, and her ability to find allies and win them over to her side proved to be instrumental in getting Kansas Speedway. While no legislators openly opposed the track itself, some questioned the government's concessions, particularly the 30-year tax abatement. While a 20-year tax abatement was allowed by current law, a 30-year tax break required the passage of a special bill.

While the project was being debated by the city council, Marinovich acknowledged the challenges it faced. "Nobody liked 30 years," she told a reporter for *The Kansas City Star* at the time. "But what if Wyandotte County and Kansas face the choice of 30 years of tax abatement or no race track? I think I know what the answer is."

One of the strong partnerships Mayor Marinovich formed was with Governor Bill Graves. The state of Kansas was critically important to the whole effort. There's no doubt that if the state had not backed the project as ardently as it did, today local racing fans might be flocking to Missouri Speedway in Jackson County.

"I would depict the process as a vehicle driving down the highway of success," says Denney, summing up the effort with an apt automotive metaphor. "There are two people at the wheel: Carol Marinovich and Bill Graves."

Like successful NASCAR drivers, Graves and Marinovich were supported by a skillful and hardworking team. Although the group is too large to name every member, a few individuals made particularly notable contributions. Dennis Hays, Wyandotte County Administrator and Hal Walker, the Unified Government's chief counsel, played important roles in the success of the project. Together they oversaw the negotiations and were the principal contacts between the Unified Government and the state, and the Unified Government and the ISC. Lt. Governor Gary Scherer filled a similar role for the state of Kansas, overseeing negotiations and a myriad of details in putting the entire package together. He was involved in the project from day-one until the day Kansas Speedway opened.

Marinovich and the Unified Government also faced opposition from some of the 150 property owners who had to be relocated from the rural, 1000-acre site near the intersection of I-70 and I-435 that had been selected as the most suitable for the speedway. Then there were the naysayers who simply were not convinced that the time, effort, financial concessions and general upheaval would be worth it in the end. "How much is it really going to help Wyandotte County," asked one undecided legislator during the debate.

Fortunately for everyone, these opinions remained in the minority and the ISC was won over – blown away! – by the county's proposal. Since then, the Speedway and Village West have, indeed, helped the county. If anything they have exceeded everyone's expectations, creating jobs, bringing in visitors and tax dollars, and turning Wyandotte County into something few people thought possible: a tourist destination.

"The total elected body deserves credit, but Carol was out front with it," Denney says. "She received the strong support that was needed, first from the city council and then from the new governing body of the Unified Government. She received unanimous support from them, which was very necessary for the project to proceed."

"With the speedway," Marinovich explained to *Governing Magazine* in 2002, "we had to work with the state of Kansas and the private components. Downtown, a unified government or neighborhood organization…cannot do it alone. You have to work on forging strong partnerships."

Special thanks to:
CitiGroup
Clarkson Construction
Gould Evans
JE Dunn Construction
Maxim Technologies
Springstead Financial
Superior Bowen Asphalt
Zimmer Real Estate Services, Inc.

NASCAR
Winston Cup Series

Ford
MIDWEST FORD DEALERS

Coors LIGHT
THE OFFICIAL BEER

KANSAS
SPEEDWAY

KANSASSP.

◀ **Curt Cavin** has covered motorsports at the *Indianapolis Star* since 1987, leading the newspaper's coverage of the Indianapolis 500, NASCAR's Brickyard 400 and Formula One's U.S. Grand Prix.

The Franklin College graduate also is the auto racing analyst for Indianapolis television station WTHR-Channel 13 and is a regular contributor to *AutoWeek Magazine*.

His work drew international attention in 2004 when he counted all 257,325 permanent seats at the Indianapolis Motor Speedway, where officials have never announced attendance figures.

◀ **Sammie Lukaskiewicz** is the public relations manager for Kansas Speedway. She is one of the original employees of the track, joining the staff in 2000. She oversees the track's media activities and acts as a liaison with race car drivers during press conferences and other functions.

Sammie is a 1993 graduate of the University of Texas at El Paso where she earned a bachelor's of arts degree in journalism. She's a former newspaper journalist, and has worked as a crime and city reporter, copy editor and page designer.

Sammie resides in Leavenworth, KS, with her husband, Bill, a U.S. Army major, and their two dogs, Winston and Frieda.

➤ **Rick Peterson** has been a sports writer for 25 years, and has been with *The Topeka Capital-Journal* in Topeka, Kansas since 1989. He has covered high school, college and professional sports in his career in addition to auto racing. He has covered virtually every major event at Kansas Speedeay and Heartland Park Topeka since those facilities opened.

Peterson has received Kansas sports writer of the year awards six times from four different organizations.

Peterson is a native of Kansas City, KS and is a graduate of Wyandotte High School and Southwestern College.

He is married (Linda) and has a son (Rickie) and a daughter (Courtney).